MW01698203

Dolch™

Forging Ahead

SRA
Columbus, OH

The McGraw·Hill Companies

Revised under the direction of the Dolch Family Trust.

SRAonline.com

SRA

Send all inquiries to:
SRA/McGraw-Hill
8787 Orion Place
Columbus, OH 43240-4027

Printed in the United States of America.

ISBN 0-07-603215-9

1 2 3 4 5 6 7 8 9 QPD 12 11 10 09 08 07 06 05 04

The McGraw-Hill Companies

Table of Contents

The Horseless Carriage

Grandfather Gersch looked out the large window. A little snow covered the houses and yards of Evanston, Illinois.

"It is only Thanksgiving Day, and we already have snow," Grandfather said.

"Not much, though," said Grandmother.

"No, not much, but enough to make people slip and slide as they walk," said Grandfather. He thought for a second that he should go outside and clear the sidewalk.

"Young Andrew will like to slip and slide in the snow," said Grandmother.

"Yes, that is true," said Grandfather with a smile. "Andrew will be happy it snowed. That boy sure likes to throw snowballs."

"And besides," said Grandmother, "you have to like winter and snow very much to live around here."

As Grandfather and Grandmother cooked Thanksgiving dinner, they talked and laughed. They were happy the family would be together today. But as they worked, Grandfather kept looking out the windows to see whether their company had come yet.

Grandmother had a smile on her face as she watched Grandfather. She knew Grandfather could not wait to see the family. She felt the same way.

On one of his many trips to the window, Grandfather at last called out, “They are here! They are here!”

Grandmother ran to the window and stood next to Grandfather. They watched as the carriage pulled up. Out of it climbed young Andrew and his mother and father.

As Andrew and Mother came up the walk, Father took the horse and carriage into the small barn behind the house. Soon the whole Gersch family was in the warm, happy home.

Andrew, Mother, and Father did not have to come far. Their house was in Evanston, too, just a short carriage ride away.

Evanston was a pretty city with many nice homes. It was even called “The City of Homes.” Some people in those homes worked in Chicago, which was just a few miles south of Evanston.

“How was the carriage ride in this snow, Andrew?” asked Grandfather.

"It was fun. I like the snow! And what fun that it has come so early this year!" said Andrew. "But I hope the snow does not make it too hard to race today."

Grandfather laughed. He had not thought about the race in a while, but Andrew could not stop thinking about it. It would be a race like none of them had ever seen before.

"Now tell me again," said Grandfather. "Is it a bicycle race? Bicycles would slip and slide on the roads today. That could be bad. I don't think I would like to watch something like that."

Andrew knew all about bicycles. He had his very own bicycle that he used to ride to school and all over the city of Evanston.

A new bicycle company had opened in Chicago just last month. Grandfather had said that next summer he would take Andrew to see how bicycles were made.

"No, Grandfather," said Andrew. Grandfather knew what race Andrew was talking about. Andrew knew Grandfather was just pulling his leg.

Before Andrew could say what kind of race it was, Grandfather asked, "An electric streetcar race?"

Andrew knew all about electric streetcars too. Just two years ago, in 1893, a streetcar line had been built to run between Chicago and Evanston. Many people who worked in Chicago now took the streetcar every day. Last summer Grandfather and Andrew had gone for a ride on one.

"No, Grandfather, not an electric streetcar race!" said Andrew. "You know I mean the automobile race!"

"Oh, yes," said Grandfather. "The horseless carriage race!"

"That is right," said Andrew. "The horseless carriage race! But I like to call it an automobile, Grandfather. *Horseless carriage* sounds so old."

Many people called the automobile the horseless carriage. That is what most automobiles looked like in 1895—a carriage without a horse. Automobiles were new machines that had been invented a few years before. It was said that the automobile would take the place of the carriage someday, but many people were still not so sure.

Andrew also knew all about automobiles. Of all the machines invented in the last several years, automobiles were the ones he knew the most about. He could not read enough about them.

"I think the automobile race could have been called off today," said Father. "Those machines were not invented for snow. The little snow we have today will make it hard for automobiles to stay on the road. They will slip and slide all over."

"Yes," said Grandfather. "And automobile engines break down in this cold weather."

"I hope the automobiles still race today," Andrew said. "If they did race, they should have started early this morning."

"It is a surprise that the race was planned for Thanksgiving Day," said Father.

"It was planned first for October, Father," said Andrew, "but not many automobiles were ready then."

A Chicago newspaper had planned the automobile race for months. The race would be 54 miles long, from the south side of Chicago to Evanston and back. At one time 89 automobiles were going to race, but they could not be ready in October. So the newspaper had said the race would be on Thanksgiving Day instead.

Of course, the newspaper did not know it would snow the day before Thanksgiving!

Andrew walked to the window. "Grandfather, what time is it now?" he asked. If the race was still going on, he wanted more than anything to see it as it turned around in Evanston.

Grandfather looked at his pocket watch. "It is almost noon, Andrew," he said. "But why should you want to know?"

Andrew was still looking out the window. "And at what time will we eat Thanksgiving dinner?" he asked as he turned to look at Grandfather.

Grandfather knew what Andrew was thinking. "In two or three hours," Grandfather said. "That big bird has to stay in the oven for a while yet."

"If the race is on, the automobiles should be in Evanston very soon—snow or no snow," Andrew said.

Grandfather and Father laughed and looked at each other. At last Father said, "Would you like to go to the race, Andrew?"

"Boy, would I!" said Andrew.

"We will ask Grandmother if we can leave the house for a bit. If she does not mind, we will see whether the automobile race is on and whether the automobiles can make it to Evanston," said Grandfather.

Grandmother did not mind, and soon Grandfather, Father, and Andrew were in Father's carriage. The horse pulled the carriage through the snow-covered streets. The weather was still very cold.

Andrew knew just where the automobiles would be in Evanston. The spot was not that far from Grandfather's house. In 15 minutes the horse had pulled the carriage to where the automobiles would turn around. A small crowd of people stood around waiting for the automobiles.

Grandfather climbed out of the carriage and asked one of the men in the crowd whether the race was on.

"Yes," said the man. He was jumping up and down to keep warm. "Only six automobiles could start in this cold weather. But they should be here very soon."

As the man spoke, the crowd heard a loud roaring sound. "Here they come!" the man said as the crowd cheered.

When Father's horse heard the roaring sound, it jumped around.

Father said to Grandfather and Andrew, "I will stay here with our horse, but you two can go get a better look."

"Thanks, Father," said Andrew.

Now the roaring sound was very loud. Grandfather and Andrew stood in the middle of the small crowd and waited. In a minute or so, they saw three automobiles.

One automobile, with the number 5 on it, was far in front of the other two. The lead automobile looked like a horseless carriage with two men in it. Andrew saw one man hold on to a stick with his hands. He used the stick to turn the wheels of the automobile.

The crowd cheered as Number 5 turned around and headed back for Chicago. In minutes the crowd cheered again as the other two automobiles made the turn.

As one automobile turned, it came to a stop. A man jumped out and tried to fix its engine. The other automobile kept going. It was trying to catch Number 5. The crowd cheered for the other automobile too.

An hour after the automobiles came to Evanston, Andrew's family ate a nice Thanksgiving dinner in Grandmother and Grandfather's warm house. The family talked about the race and automobiles. Grandmother and Mother had heard the engines from the house!

"Well, Andrew," said Grandfather. "There might be something to this horseless carriage of yours."

"Yes, Grandfather," said Andrew. "And who knows? Maybe someday we will come to your house for Thanksgiving in an automobile."

Can They Stay in Clinton?

On a fall day in the year 1900, Adie sat with her book on the rocks near the Mississippi River. The town of Clinton, Iowa, seemed quiet today. And it was quiet!

Two or three years ago Clinton had been full of noise and people. Adie remembered those days well. Clinton had been a city of busy sawmills then. Now it was a city of empty sawmills.

When the sawmills had been busy, Adie's father and many, many other men had worked in them. The men had worked long hours, but they had made a lot of money.

Adie tried to read her book as she sat on the rocks, but reading was hard because she was sad. Instead of reading, she kept remembering the days when the sawmills had been busy.

The air in Clinton had been filled with smoke, dust, and noise then, which was a bad thing about the mills. Now the air was clear, and the city was quiet.

But some things about the mills had been very good. The sawmills' large saws had cut logs from Minnesota into lumber. The lumber had been made into everything—houses, barns, stores, other buildings, furniture, boats, and much more.

Some of the lumber had stayed in Clinton, but most of it had been sold to places west of Iowa, where houses and towns were springing up everywhere. The sawmills had sold a lot of lumber, made a lot of money, and helped Clinton, Iowa, grow into a rich town in only a few short years.

For the Clinton sawmills to stay busy, they had needed one important thing: logs. The logs the sawmills cut into lumber had come from the large forests of Minnesota to the north.

Lumberjacks would cut down trees and roll logs into the Mississippi River or into rivers that led to the Mississippi River. The logs would then float down the Mississippi. Boats would make sure the logs floated to Clinton and to the sawmills.

Adie had often watched the logs come down the river and into Clinton. She had always been surprised by how big the logs were.

To Adie, the river seemed as though it would always be full of logs for the sawmills. But Minnesota only had so many trees and forests.

As lumberjacks had cut and cut, Minnesota had run out of trees and forests. Around 1899, lumberjacks had no trees left to cut. No logs floated down the Mississippi.

The sawmills in Clinton had run out of logs to cut into lumber. One sawmill company after another had had to close. There was no work to do.

One day Father had come home early and talked to Mother, Adie, and her big brother Aaron in the kitchen.

"The sawmill shut down today," he had said. "I am out of work. Most of the men in town are out of work too."

Adie and Aaron had never seen their father look so sad.

"What will we do?" Adie had asked.

"I will look for other work in Clinton," Father had said.

"We will all find work to do in Clinton. We will all help," Mother had said.

"If we do not find any other work, we may have to move to a new town that has sawmills and enough logs for those sawmills," Father had said.

Adie had not wanted to move. She had not wanted the family to leave Clinton. Adie knew Clinton was a good place for a family to live. And she was old enough to know other places might not be as nice, even if those places had work for Father.

At first Father had found many little jobs to make money. Mother had too. But it was hard. Many other people in Clinton had been looking for little jobs to do as well.

In just a short time after the sawmills had shut down, many, many people had left Clinton because they could find only little jobs and no real work.

So many people had left Clinton that soon there were more than just empty sawmills in town. There were many empty houses up and down the streets as well.

Father had thought there might be more real work then for the people who stayed, but that had not been true. For the last two years Father, Mother, Adie, and Aaron had had to be careful to save every penny.

Now in the fall of 1900, it looked as though the family would have to move from Clinton too. Father could find no real work. He and Mother could not even find little jobs. It seemed that Clinton and its people would never get back on their feet again.

On this fall day, Adie shut her book and stood up by the river. It was too sad thinking about the past.

Adie knew her family would have to leave Clinton soon. It did her no good to feel bad about it. Adie would just have to make the best of the move. And her whole family would have to make the best of it too.

As Adie walked home, she looked at all the empty sawmills along the river. Their tall, quiet chimneys reached into the sky.

Adie walked more and passed a very nice neighborhood in the center of town. Many people who owned the sawmills had built these large houses. The houses were beautiful, but many of them were empty.

Then Adie walked through her neighborhood. The houses were not as big as the houses in the other neighborhood, but they were still nice. Adie loved her neighborhood and would miss it.

Then Adie saw her big brother Aaron walking in front of her. He had his newspapers with him. Aaron sold newspapers to make money for the family.

"Aaron, wait for me," she called as she ran to catch up with him.

Aaron heard Adie and waited for her. "I did not sell all my newspapers today. We can read one at home," he said.

"May I read it as we walk?" she asked. Adie liked to read the newspaper whenever she had the chance.

"Sure," said Aaron with a smile. Aaron knew Adie loved to read.

Across the front page of the newspaper were the words "Carnegie to Build Public Library in Clinton."

Adie loved books, but the news made her sad. It would be great news if the family were staying in Clinton. But Adie did not think the family would be there when the public library was built.

Still, Adie read the story as she and Aaron walked home. As she read, she started to smile. She had been wrong. This might be very good news after all!

"Did you read about the library?" Adie asked Aaron. She had a bright smile on her face that Aaron had not seen in quite a while.

"Not yet," said Aaron. But he could tell Adie wanted him to read it, so he did as he walked.

After he read the story, he and Adie started to run home. They could not wait to tell Father and Mother what the story said about the new library.

The newspaper story was about Andrew Carnegie. Few people in the United States or in the world were as rich as Andrew Carnegie. He had started with almost nothing, but with hard work, he had made much money.

Carnegie had made most of his money through the Carnegie Steel Company. He knew that strong steel would be needed as people built new machines all over the United States and the world. As more train tracks, buildings, and large sailing ships were built, more of Carnegie's steel mills began to spring up. The mills made most of the steel for the country and did very, very well.

But Andrew Carnegie did not just make money. Few people gave away more money than he. One way Andrew Carnegie gave away money was to build public library after public library in town after town across America.

Adie already knew Andrew Carnegie built many a library. She had often wondered whether he would pay to have a library built in Clinton. But the newspaper story told her something she did not know.

When Adie and Aaron got home, they told Father and Mother all about the new library. As they talked, a big smile crossed Father's face. "I see why you two are happy about the library," he said. "They will need good people to build the library—people like me!"

"That is a big reason we are happy," said Aaron.

"But we are happy for another reason too," said Adie. "Andrew Carnegie will only build a library in a town that can pay to take care of the library as the years go by."

"And the newspaper said that Andrew Carnegie thinks Clinton can pay to take care of the library, even with the sawmills shut down," said Aaron.

"He is a bright man," said Mother. "He must know something about Clinton."

“The newspaper says Clinton will soon be a city of busy grain mills,” said Adie.

Grain mills would turn corn into other products. The products would be sold. The products would help the people in Clinton make money again.

“We will stay in Clinton!” said Father.

The next day Adie sat on the rocks and looked at the empty sawmills. They would soon be gone from Clinton. But her family would stay, and Adie was happy.

Waiting for Mr. Hardy

Days in a lighthouse were never easy, no matter where the lighthouse was.

The family who ran the lighthouse was often alone for a very long time. The family had to work hard all day and every day. Just climbing the many steps to the lamp at the top of the lighthouse was hard work. There could be hundreds of steps! And the family was always worried.

They were worried for a good reason. A lighthouse was built to make sure ships stayed away from danger. A lighthouse told a ship's captain that danger of one kind or another was near.

That is why a family who ran a lighthouse worried. They worried that a ship's captain at sea might not see the lighthouse in time. Or they worried that the big lamp at the top of the lighthouse would go out and that the captain would not even know danger was near.

Most of all, the family worried that shipwrecks might take place if things went wrong.

The Coates family ran a lighthouse on the outer banks of North Carolina. The danger for ships around their lighthouse was sand.

Many of the outer banks were long islands of sand. In the right weather or at the right time of day, ship captains could not see the sand. And some of the sand banks would move from one place to another. A ship's captain could never know where the sand banks were. So ships were always in danger because they might hit the sand.

The outer banks' lighthouses made sure ships stayed away from the sand. And the lighthouses did their jobs well. Before 1903 when no lighthouses were on the outer banks, there were many shipwrecks. But after the lighthouses were built on the outer banks, there were few shipwrecks around the islands.

The Coates family was glad there were few shipwrecks. It meant they were doing their job very well. Mr. Coates was the lighthouse keeper. But the whole family, Mrs. Coates, Ben, Rosie, and Johnny, all worked in the lighthouse.

The keeper and his family were always busy. Not only did they do lighthouse work, but they were all part of the lighthouse school too. Mr. and Mrs. Coates did the teaching, and the three children did the learning. Ben, Rosie, and Johnny lived too far from any other school in North Carolina to think of going elsewhere. And besides, they were often needed to help their mother and father around the lighthouse.

At times the Coates family missed seeing other people. But most of the time they loved their work. There was always something new to see on the outer banks. The Atlantic Ocean and the sky above it looked different from day to day. On some days they looked different from hour to hour.

Ben always said, "We live in the most beautiful place in the world! The water and the sky are so pretty."

Rosie always said, "It is nice being a lighthouse keeper's family. I would not want to live anywhere else."

Johnny always said, "When will the inspector come?"

The whole family wondered that too. Except for shipwrecks, they worried most about Mr. Hardy, the lighthouse inspector. But they did not know when or if he would come to their lighthouse.

Every lighthouse keeper's family worried about Mr. Hardy. But they knew the inspector had to do his job too.

Mr. Hardy checked that the lamp on the lighthouse worked well. He also checked that the windows around the lamp were clean. A working lamp and clean windows were the most important things a lighthouse could have.

But it was the other little things Mr. Hardy checked that the family worried about. While wearing white gloves, he checked for dirt all over the lighthouse and in the keeper's house. The inspector's gloves ran over doors, windows, walls, tables, chairs, and the chimney. If he found dust or dirt on his gloves, he might get very angry!

Mr. Hardy also checked for bugs and animals in the house. He checked to make sure the paint on the lighthouse was fresh. He checked everything!

The family had heard story after story about the lighthouse inspector. Other families had said he would fire a lighthouse keeper on the spot if something were not clean. The families had said that if anything at all were wrong, Mr. Hardy would find it.

It had also been said that Mr. Hardy was proud of his strong eyesight. From high on top of a lighthouse he could see dirt on a porch far below. But he did not use his strong eyesight just to see dirt. Mr. Hardy loved to spot rare birds.

Mr. Hardy loved rare birds so much that he always had two books about the birds with him. One book told all about the birds—what their names were, what they looked like, and where they could be found. Mr. Hardy used the other book to keep track of the birds he saw in the wild. In the little book, he would write the names of the birds he saw and the places he saw them.

Sometimes if a lighthouse had only a little bit of dirt and Mr. Hardy saw a rare bird around the lighthouse, he would not be so hard on the family. He would be so proud of his strong eyesight and of finding a new bird that he would forget about a little bit of dust or dirt. Some lighthouse families even kept rare birds around just so Mr. Hardy would spot them.

Mr. and Mrs. Coates would never keep a rare bird for Mr. Hardy. They did not think it would be fair to the rare bird. And they wanted Mr. Hardy to see all the hard, careful work they had done.

So the family cleaned, washed, painted, and picked up all the time, just in case Mr. Hardy came. They would have taken care of the lighthouse even if they thought Mr. Hardy would never come.

After the family cleaned everything, Mr. Coates would put on white gloves and check everything in the same way Mr. Hardy would.

Once in a while, Mr. Coates would get a bit of dust or dirt on his gloves, but not often. His lighthouse was very clean, and that made him proud.

After a while, it seemed as though Mr. Hardy would never come. The Coates family ran the lighthouse for many years, and the inspector and his white gloves never came.

Johnny started saying, "I do not think there is a real inspector named Mr. Hardy. It is just a story people tell us so we will keep everything clean."

Everyone in the Coates family began to think Johnny's words must be true. But in December 1903, they found out they were wrong.

The family found out Mr. Hardy was real when he knocked on their door as the sun came up one morning. “I am Mr. Hardy, the lighthouse inspector,” he said as he put a white glove on each hand.

The Coates family was worried. They had cleaned the house yesterday, as they did every day. But it was too early to clean the house yet today.

Would Mr. Hardy find any dust or dirt? It seemed as though he was trying very hard to do just that!

He started in the Coates's house. He ran his white gloves along everything in the house. As he did, he checked his gloves over and over. But he found nothing.

Then Mr. Hardy checked the outside of the house. He found nothing. He checked the outside of the lighthouse. He found nothing. He checked the door to the lighthouse, inside and out. He still found nothing.

Then Mr. Hardy climbed up the many, many steps that led to the lighthouse lamps. He checked every step as he climbed. He found nothing. He checked the railing next to the steps. He found nothing—until he got to the very top of the railing.

At the top of the railing Mr. Hardy found a bit of dust. He said, "My, my."

Then Mr. Hardy showed the dust on his white gloves to the Coates family. Now the family wished more than anything that they had a rare bird flying around the lighthouse. It would help!

Mr. Hardy put on another pair of clean white gloves. He checked the lamp. He found nothing. He checked the windows. Before he got very far, he found something. But it was not dirt. It was a rare bird he saw out the window.

"I have never seen a bird that big!" said Mr. Hardy pointing to one of the islands on the outer banks. "I have never seen a bird fly like that."

As quick as can be, Mr. Hardy pulled out his book about rare birds and thumbed through the pages to find this big, strange bird. He could find nothing like it in the book. Mr. Hardy could not believe it. He had found a bird no one had ever seen!

In seconds the bird was gone, but Mr. Hardy was proud and happy. He forgot about the dirt on his gloves. He told the Coates family they were doing a fine job, and he left!

The Coates family wondered what kind of bird Mr. Hardy had seen. Two weeks after the inspector's visit, the Coates family read a story in the newspaper. The story was about two brothers, Orville and Wilbur Wright. They had made a flying machine and had tried to fly it at Kitty Hawk on the outer banks. They had tried to fly it on December 17, the day Mr. Hardy had been at the Coates's lighthouse.

Mr. Hardy had seen something rare, but he had not seen a bird. He had seen the first airplane!

Too Much Excitement!

Mr. James W. Campion was a tall, quiet man. He did not care much for excitement. It was a wonder that such a quiet man would live in a place as busy as New York City in 1904. His friends always told him he should move to a small town in the country. But he never did. New York City was his home.

Still Mr. Campion tried to live without too much excitement. He had a job in a quiet office. His walk to and from work was short and quiet, even though it was in a busy part of New York City.

Mr. Campion did not even read the newspapers. They were full of just too much excitement.

One evening Mr. Campion was walking from work to his home. His walk was quiet until he turned a corner into Columbus Circle. This was the one part of his walk home that Mr. Campion did not like.

Columbus Circle could be full of people, and this evening it was. Mr. Campion saw a very big crowd of people. "Oh, no!" he thought.

Mr. Campion turned around to take the long way home. He wanted to miss the crowd and the excitement in Columbus Circle. But as he turned, he saw even more people walking to Columbus Circle. And they were all walking to the very big crowd.

So many people were going that way that Mr. Campion had to go with them, whether he wanted to or not. And he did not want to! He was pushed along by the people and soon was part of the very big crowd. This crowd was moving, too, and with it, Mr. Campion was moving.

The men, women, and children in the crowd all talked and laughed. They all walked fast, as if they could not wait to get where they were going. And they all pushed Mr. Campion to where they were going. But Mr. Campion had no idea where that was! All he knew was that this was too much excitement.

The crowd kept moving and pushing Mr. Campion along with it. Mr. Campion was tall enough to see over the heads of many people in the crowd. He looked all around to find a way out of the crowd. He could not see one.

Then Mr. Campion looked in front of him to see where the crowd was going. At first he could not see anything. He still had no idea where the crowd was going.

Then on the other side of Columbus Circle he saw a strange little building.

Mr. Campion had often seen the strange little building as he walked to and from work. And he did wonder what the building was, but he had never gone to find out.

Now, as he moved with the crowd, he remembered that the strange little building was built in the shape of a triangle. The triangle had a wide door on one side. The crowd was headed to the wide door in the triangle. And so was Mr. Campion, very much against his will.

Where did the wide door go? What was the crowd going to see or do? What in the world was Mr. Campion going to do? He had no idea!

As the crowd moved closer and closer to the wide door, the people started to slow down. There were too many people in the crowd to fit through the door at once. When the crowd got even closer to the door, the people could not move at all.

The people in the crowd—and Mr. Campion—would have to wait their turns to go through the wide door. But Mr. Campion did not want a turn! This was too much excitement.

With the crowd stopped for a few minutes, Mr. Campion started to hear what some people were talking about. He heard mothers and fathers telling large families of children different things.

"Remember, do not put your heads out the windows," said one mother to her family. "You could be hurt."

"Yes," said the family's father. "And do not put your hands out the windows either."

Mr. Campion wondered what that meant. Where was the crowd going that had windows? And was there a chance he could get hurt?

"Oh, my," Mr. Campion whispered to himself. His heart began to pound more and more.

"Do not write on the walls," said a father to his family. "The good people who built it might not like that very much."

Mr. Campion wondered what that meant too. Who would ever write on walls? Then he thought, "We are going to a place with windows and walls."

"Do not open a door and walk into the next car," said a big sister to her family. "I read that all people who ride are to stay in their seats at all times."

Now Mr. Campion knew what the people were talking about. Windows, walls, doors, seats, and cars were all parts of a train. And a train was something many people could ride at once.

That was it! The crowd was going on a train. Had there always been a train that went through Columbus Circle? Where were the tracks? Mr. Campion did not like the excitement of a train ride!

Tall Mr. Campion again looked all around for a way out of the crowd. He still could not find one. What could he do? His mind began to race, and his heart still pounded. He just wanted to get home!

As he stood and waited to be pushed through the wide door in the triangle-shaped building, he now heard several children in the crowd asking their mothers and fathers questions.

“How fast will it go?” asked a little girl. She did not seem afraid of the crowd or the train.

“It will go about 45 miles an hour,” said her father.

“Oh, no,” thought Mr. Campion. “I do not want to go that fast. That is way too much excitement!”

“What if there is an accident?” asked a little boy.

“There will not be an accident,” said the boy’s mother. “The story in the newspaper said not to worry about that.”

“Accident!” thought Mr. Campion. Now he tried even harder to turn around and get out of the crowd.

But just then, the people around Mr. Campion started moving again. They were going through the wide door in the strange little building, and Mr. Campion was going with them!

Now Mr. Campion worried about something new. How would all the people in the crowd fit into the little building? As soon as he moved through the door, tall Mr. Campion saw the answer.

Just inside the wide door were stairs. The crowd walked down the stairs, and so did Mr. Campion. He was in no danger of falling down the stairs—too many people were in front of him!

The stairs went very deep under the ground, and then they turned and went down even deeper. The crowd followed the stairs down, made the turn, and then went deeper too. So did Mr. Campion.

But Mr. Campion did not want to go deeper. He wanted to go back up. He was finding it very hard to get enough air and was feeling quite light-headed.

In a few minutes the crowd was on a platform. Tall Mr. Campion saw that next to the platform were what looked like railroad tracks. Here, deep below New York City, was where trains would run as fast as 45 miles an hour.

On the platform, the crowd pushed to a window. All the people in the crowd bought tickets at the window.

When the crowd pushed Mr. Campion to the window, a man behind the window said, "A nickel."

Mr. Campion did not do anything. The man said again, “A nickel!”

Mr. Campion did not want any excitement at the window, so he gave the man a nickel and bought a ticket.

As the crowd pushed Mr. Campion away from the window, a train raced up next to the platform. People on the platform began to step onto the train. Then the train raced away. It raced too fast!

The crowd pushed more, but Mr. Campion had made up his mind. He was not going on the train!

Mr. Campion looked around and saw a policeman on the platform. Mr. Campion started to wave. The policeman saw him and knew Mr. Campion wanted help. The policeman walked into the crowd and pulled Mr. Campion out.

“This is too much excitement!” said Mr. Campion.

The policeman had seen a few people like Mr. Campion in the subway that night. He led Mr. Campion to the stairs that went up, not down.

When Mr. Campion was above the ground again and out of the building in the shape of a triangle, he ran from Columbus Circle. On his way home, he bought a newspaper for the first time in months. The newspaper said, "First New York City Subway to Open Tonight."

"A new subway," thought Mr. Campion. "From now on I must buy a newspaper every day. It will help me miss the excitement!"

A Big Story

On the morning of April 18, 1906, the newspaper office in Chicago was almost empty and all was quiet. Most of the reporters were gone. It was often this way in the early morning.

The day's newspaper was already being sold on the streets of Chicago. The reporters who had put it together were now at home in bed. But in a few hours, they would come back to the office and start to get tomorrow's newspaper ready.

But Stella Walsh was already in the office. She had a lot to do in the mornings. Part of her job was to begin to get the next day's newspaper ready. Another part was to be in the office in case big news came across the telegraph line.

At about 7:45 that morning, a strange message came over the telegraph line. It was from far away in Germany. The message said a big earthquake had hit California.

"That is not right," thought Stella. "How can people in Germany know about an earthquake thousands and thousands of miles away?"

Stella looked at the message for a minute or two. If big news came over the telegraph line, Stella had to send out a message about that big news. She had to send the message to the man who ran the newspaper, Arthur J. Kranz.

Mr. Kranz wanted to know right away when big news—but only big news—came over the telegraph line. Small news could wait until he came into the office late in the morning. Mr. Kranz did not like to wake up early for no reason!

Was the news about the earthquake big news? Stella was not sure. Then another message came across the telegraph line. This *was* big news. The message said that at 5:13 that morning in California, a large earthquake had hit the city of San Francisco.

Stella looked at her watch. The time in San Francisco was different than in Chicago. When the earthquake took place at 5:13 in the morning in California, it was 7:13 in the morning in Chicago.

The message from Germany had come about a half hour after the earthquake hit. How did people in Germany know? Could they feel the earthquake as far away as Germany?

Stella could not find out the answers to those questions now. She had to make sure Mr. Kranz knew what was going on in San Francisco. This was big news—big enough to wake Mr. Kranz!

Stella could use the telephone to call Mr. Kranz's house. The telephone was still pretty new in 1906. Telephone lines did not reach all across America or the world yet, and few people had them.

No telephone lines ran from Chicago to San Francisco, but one line ran from the newspaper office in Chicago to Mr. Kranz's big house in Chicago. Mr. Kranz was an important man and one of the few people in town who had the money to buy a telephone.

Mr. Kranz was slow to answer the telephone. When he did, Stella could tell he had been sleeping.

"Mr. Kranz, I wanted you to know that a big earthquake hit San Francisco about an hour ago," said Stella.

"How big?" asked Mr. Kranz.

"So big that people thousands of miles away in the country of Germany know about it," said Stella.

Mr. Kranz was quiet for a few seconds. Then he said, "I will be there in an hour or so. Thank you for the call, Stella."

As Stella hung up the telephone, the telegraph line was busy again. A message came from the state of Oregon, north of California. People in Oregon had felt the earthquake.

Then a message came from the state of Nevada, west of the state of California. People had felt the earthquake there too. A message also came from Los Angeles, south of San Francisco. People had felt the earthquake there as well!

This had been a big earthquake!

After the message from Los Angeles, the telegraph line was quiet for a little while. Stella wondered whether the earthquake had brought down the telegraph lines.

But in minutes, the telegraph was busy again. As Stella read the message, she got another surprise. This message was from New York City. It said all the telegraph lines that ran from San Francisco to the East were down. But one line still ran under the Pacific Ocean. Messages sent on that line would go to India and then to New York City.

About 9:00 in the morning Mr. Kranz came into the newspaper office wearing a dark wool suit and his black hat on his head. He always wore the black hat when there was a big news story.

Mr. Kranz was standing next to Stella when the next telegraph message came from New York City. It said that many, many buildings in San Francisco had come down in the terrible earthquake. Many people were hurt.

Then Mr. Kranz read all the messages from that morning. "You were right, Stella. This is bad news," he said.

Mr. Kranz then told Stella to get in touch with all the reporters who worked at the newspaper. He wanted them to come to the office right away. They needed to come so they could write stories about the big, terrible earthquake for the next day's paper.

As Stella made telephone calls, more telegraph messages started to come from New York City.

The first message had more terrible news. The earthquake had started both electric and gas fires. Stella knew electric and gas fires were hard to put out. It was hard to turn off a city's gas after an earthquake.

The next telegraph message said that United States soldiers were being sent to San Francisco to help the people there. It also said that much of San Francisco had been destroyed.

The earthquake had destroyed a lot of the city, but fire had destroyed even more. And the firefighters had no way to put out the large fires!

Soon the newspaper office in Chicago started to fill with reporters. As they came into the office and heard the story about the earthquake, they could not believe it. It was hard to think something so terrible had happened.

More messages and reporters came into the newspaper office. When all the reporters were there, Mr. Kranz asked them to come to a quick meeting in his office.

"The earthquake in San Francisco is a big story. We must tell the story as well as we can for the people of Chicago," said Mr. Kranz.

Then Mr. Kranz took off his hat. He set it on his desk with the open end up. He said, "This is a big hat. We must fill it with money to help the people of San Francisco."

Then Mr. Kranz put a one-hundred-dollar bill into the hat. The reporters put money in the hat too. They did not make as much money as Mr. Kranz, but they gave all they could.

Over the next several days, as the reporters learned more and more about what had happened in the earthquake, they filled the hat over and over with money for the people of San Francisco. These poor people would need all the money they could get to build their lives again.

All that first day Stella stayed near the telegraph and took more messages. She kept very busy. There were many messages from all over the world.

Another message came from Germany. It said there was a machine in Germany that measured earthquakes all around the world. Now Stella knew why the first telegraph message about San Francisco had come from Germany.

That morning the machine in Germany had measured the earthquake in San Francisco. It was a very, very strong one. It was the kind of earthquake that only happened about once every two hundred years.

Other machines all over the world had also measured the San Francisco earthquake. They all showed the same thing. That morning's earthquake had been the most terrible in years.

The reporters worked hard all day to find out what happened in San Francisco. The people of Chicago wanted to know everything they could.

Late in the afternoon, the reporters started to write stories for the next day's paper. The stories were sad for the reporters to write. The stories would be sad for the people of Chicago to read.

The fire in San Francisco burned for three days. Most people there lost everything they owned.

Stella stayed in the office for almost three days in a row. Most of the reporters did too. And Mr. Kranz stayed in the office quite a lot as well. They passed the days eating, sleeping, and working.

When Stella walked home at last, she thought about how the people of Chicago had made their city even better after the Great Fire of 1871.

Stella knew the people of San Francisco would make their city better too.

She also knew that all over the city of Chicago, people were filling hats with money for the people of San Francisco.

Three Cheers for Pa

It had been a difficult several months. And that was a surprise.

The family had thought that when Pa came back from the war, life would be the way it was before he left. That did not mean life would be easy. Life was never easy on a Texas farm.

But the family had expected Pa to be the same man he was before the war. They had expected life to be the same. They had expected to be happy again.

When Pa had been a United States soldier fighting for the army in the Great War in France, all Ma and the children could do was wait and hope he would come home soon. Those times had been the most difficult.

For many weeks in a row, the family would not hear from or about Pa. They had worried very, very much. Then they would get many letters from him all at once. Pa had tried to write every day and often did.

Letters just did not get to America very fast while the fighting went on in France.

After a little while, the family had learned that Pa's letters would not always come very fast. Of course, they still worried very much when they did not hear from Pa, but they now knew the mail was just slow.

Then one terrible day, a telegraph message had come from the United States army. The message had said Pa had been hurt in France and that his injury was serious. Pa had been sent to England and would have good care there.

Ma and the children had not been told how serious the injury was. The army had not told them. Ma had cried, and the children had cried. They had been afraid and very worried.

But in a few days, a letter had come from England—a letter from Pa! He had told the family he had been hurt but that his injury was not too serious.

Pa had also said he had good care in England and would be fine. Best of all, Pa would be home soon.

When the family had read this letter, they had cried again. But this time they had cried because they were happy. Pa was fine and would be home soon!

Just two months after that, the newspapers had been full of good news. The Great War was over!

On November 11, 1918, the war had ended. Soldiers from the United States and from places all over the world could go home to their families. People had said that the Great War was so terrible that there would never be another war again!

On that day in November 1918 when the war ended, Pa had been in a ship crossing the great Atlantic Ocean. On the ship Pa had cheered when he heard the good news. All the soldiers going home on the ship had cheered. They could not wait to see their families and friends again.

In a few days Pa's ship had landed in New York Harbor. Because of his injury, other soldiers had had to help him get on a train in New York. The train would take Pa hundreds and hundreds of miles across the country, back to his family in Texas.

On November 19, 1918, Pa's family had stood in the train station in a town near their Texas farm, waiting for Pa's train from New York. Many other families had waited for their fathers too.

Ma and the children had been happy. They had thought the good life the family knew before the war could start again. They had thought the hard times were over for good.

Then the loud train had pulled into the station. The family could not wait to see Pa. As they watched, many soldiers had walked off the train into the waiting arms of their families, but they did not see Pa. Ma had been just about to go on the train to see whether he was there when she saw him.

Two soldiers had had to help Pa get off the train. Pa's injury was serious, more serious than he had said in his letter. He could not walk alone! The injury was so serious that Pa was in a wheelchair.

That happy day at the train station had turned into a time of tears for Ma, Pa, and the children. They had many sad feelings for weeks to come. For one thing, the children could not bear to see their father hurt so much. They found it hard not to cry when they saw the wheelchair. But that day the tears were not because Pa was hurt. They were because Pa was home. All the worry they had felt had built up inside them. It had been waiting to come out, and it did.

It had been hard to get Pa from the train station to the farm. The wheelchair was so big and heavy. But Ma and the two big children in the family had been strong enough to get Pa into the wagon and home at last.

Over the next few days, the family had learned just how serious Pa's injury was. He might never walk again. But Pa had said he would. Pa had said he would walk no matter what.

Even though Pa had said that, no one—not Pa, his doctors, or the family—knew for sure what would happen. Would he walk again? Would his life be anything like it had been before?

Pa must have been very sad when he came home to the farm. He must have thought about how strong he was before the war. He must have thought about how hard he could work before the war.

But if he had thought these things, Pa had not said them. If he was worried about what might happen, he had not let it show for a second.

Some of Pa's good friends had come to the farm to make some changes to the house so Pa could get around in the wheelchair. Pa had helped make the changes too.

Pa had hammered nails and sawed wood. He had even hammered better than his friends. This was something Pa could still do!

Pa had even laughed and told his friends he had always hammered better than they did! His family's hearts were not quite so heavy when they heard Pa laugh again.

In December Pa had started to work to make his legs strong again. Ma had helped him do exercises in the wheelchair. The exercises were difficult. Pa's legs had hurt very much, but he did the exercises over and over and would not give up.

By February Pa had started standing. He could not stand for long, but he had made a start. Feelings of hope had started to take the place of the family's tears.

The day Pa first stood, he had told his family how lucky he was. He had said that so many soldiers were hurt bad enough that they would never walk again, no matter how hard they tried. They had not been lucky.

Pa had said that whether or not he walked, he would always help the soldiers who could not. He would try not to think of himself when others might need him. The children looked up to their father even more when he said this.

Even with his exercises, it had been months before Pa could take a first step without falling. He had done it at last on a warm spring day in May.

Now it was June, and the town near the family's farm was going to have a Fourth of July parade. There would be bands and horses and automobiles carrying all the important people in the town.

The town asked all the soldiers from the Great War to march in the parade. Pa wanted to march, but on that day he could not yet walk more than a few steps. He was in the parade in his wheelchair.

As the people on the sidewalks cheered for the soldiers in the parade, Pa thought about how lucky he was to be there. He would not feel sorry for himself.

There would be another parade that year. It would be on November 11, 1919. On that day the United States would celebrate the end of the war. And from that day on, November 11 would always be a day to celebrate the end of wars. It would also be a day to celebrate the soldiers who had been in the wars.

Pa was sure he would march in the November parade.

By August Pa could take more than just a few steps. He needed a cane to help him. Pa did not tell the family how much his legs hurt as he took those steps. At times, though, Ma could see the pain in his eyes.

In September Pa could take many more steps with the cane. He walked so much that he wore a brown path in the grass between the house and the barn. His legs still hurt, but they were better. He again and again told his family how lucky he was. Other soldiers would never have the chance to get better.

On November 11, 1919, Pa was ready to march with the other soldiers from the Great War. The parade was to be a mile long. Pa had not yet walked that far with a cane, but he would try today. He would try for himself, for his family, and for all the soldiers who could not walk.

The day of the parade was hot for November—even in Texas. It was hard for Pa to walk a mile with the sun beating down on him. His legs hurt, and his arm hurt from the cane. But as he walked, Pa thought about how lucky he was and about how many soldiers would not get this chance.

Pa looked at all the people who watched the parade and cheered. And he saw the family who loved him standing in the crowd. "Three cheers for Pa!" they shouted. Before he knew it, Pa had marched the whole mile!

When Pa found his family again after the parade, he had a big smile on his face, and Ma knew the difficult times would soon be over. Pa would march in the parade next year, he said—and he would do it without his cane!

Looking for Charlie Chaplin

Miguel had waited for Thursday all week. But he still had a few hours until it was time to go, so he sat and played a sad song on his violin.

Miguel had been playing the violin for many years. He had learned to play when he was just a boy. He still remembered the long hours with his grandmother as she had shown him how to place his fingers over the strings and move the bow with his other hand.

Often when Miguel felt sad or angry about something, he would sit and play his violin. It always made him feel better. The soft sound of the bow against the strings made him feel calm. It could make him feel so calm that as he played, he did not worry about a thing. The music would carry him away from his problems.

When he was young, Miguel's mother would listen to his sad violin music and wonder how it could calm him so. It always made her cry.

"The music is just so beautiful, Miguel," his mother would say. Now when his mother came to visit him, she would always ask him to play for her.

Miguel looked at the clock. It was time to go. Thursday was the big opening day of a new moving picture.

Many new movies opened every week in the early 1920s, and Miguel saw a lot of them. Sometimes he would go more than one night a week!

The movies Miguel loved the most were those with a man called Charlie Chaplin. Charlie Chaplin's movies were always so funny. Miguel would watch movies of all kinds, funny or not. But he liked Charlie Chaplin movies the best!

In his black hat, dirty topcoat, and big black shoes, Charlie Chaplin was sure to make people laugh. He also had a funny walk and made a lot of funny faces.

So far, Miguel's favorite Charlie Chaplin movie was one he had seen a few years ago called *The Kid*. In it, Charlie Chaplin played a man who finds a baby and brings the little boy up as his own child. Miguel had laughed until he had tears in his eyes as he watched the little boy walk and act just like Charlie Chaplin.

Miguel put his violin back in its case, put on his coat, and left his house to go see the new moving picture. It was just a short walk down the street, but Miguel ran to the theater. He wanted to make sure he got a good seat. And he did not want to miss a second of the moving picture.

Miguel got to the theater in good time. He loved going to the movie theater. All the people who went to the theater were always dressed up, so it felt like something special was going on. And today was very special. Miguel would see the new Charlie Chaplin movie.

As he found his seat, Miguel looked around the big theater. He sat in his soft, red seat and looked out at the ocean of red seats behind and in front of him. Men who worked for the theater were dressed in red suits with red hats. These men showed many of the people to their seats.

Soon the lights in the theater went down and then back up, then down and back up again. This was the sign that the movie was about to begin and that people should find their seats. Miguel knew this was a special night because not one seat in the whole theater was empty.

The lights went down for good, and a piano player started playing. Moving pictures in the early 1920s did not have any sound. They were called silent movies. So each movie theater had a piano player who would play along with the movie.

Then Charlie Chaplin, in his black hat and suit, was on the screen in front of Miguel. After all the movies he had seen, Miguel was still surprised every time he saw people and things moving on a big screen. He had heard that the people who went to the very first movies more than twenty years ago had been quite surprised—even afraid—when they had seen the moving pictures. They had thought a train or an automobile moving on the screen would somehow come out of the screen and hit them!

That night's movie was called *The Gold Rush*. Miguel watched with a smile as Charlie Chaplin went to the cold lands of Alaska to look for gold. Charlie did all kinds of funny things in the movie. He tried to eat his leather shoe when he was hungry. And then he put two forks in two potatoes and made them look like feet that danced.

Miguel laughed and laughed at the silent movie. He thought about how much fun Charlie Chaplin must have when he made his movies. All at once Miguel knew what he wanted to do with his life. He wanted to move to Hollywood and make silent movies.

Miguel had never felt so sure about anything in his whole life. He was going to save his money and move to Hollywood in Los Angeles, California. He had seen so many movies that he was sure he could act in them.

When the movie ended and the piano player did not play anymore, Miguel walked home. He thought about how he would move to Hollywood.

As the weeks went by, Miguel soon saw that it would not be easy to go to Hollywood. He had to work hard and save all his money. And Miguel's mother was not sure that going to California to be an actor was the best thing for him to do. But still, when Miguel left for Hollywood at last, she told him he was right to follow his dream.

In Hollywood Miguel found a place to live and started to look for a job as an actor. He went to the first movie studio he could find.

"I am here to be an actor," Miguel said to a man behind a big desk. The man looked at Miguel and did not say a word. "I would like to work in Charlie Chaplin movies," Miguel said.

"Charlie Chaplin does not make his movies at this studio," the man said to Miguel. "And we do not need an actor right now."

Miguel then walked in the hot California sun to find the next movie studio. He had on his best suit and looked very good, but his suit was not made for the hot weather. Still he walked and found his way to another movie studio.

"Hello, I am here to get a job as an actor," he said to a woman behind a desk. "I would like to work with Charlie Chaplin in his next movie."

The woman looked up and down at Miguel. "I am sorry," she said with a smile. "But Charlie Chaplin does not make his movies at this studio. We also do not need an actor right now."

Miguel was not happy with how his job hunt was going so far. It was early though, he told himself, and he would keep looking.

Over the next few days, Miguel went to studio after studio. Soon he had no place left to go. Miguel had gone to every movie studio he could find, but not one needed an actor. On top of that, not one of them was the studio where Charlie Chaplin made his movies.

Then one night after a long day of walking, Miguel made his way back to his two-room Hollywood apartment. He missed his old town and friends. As he walked up the stairs he wondered how long he could pay for the apartment if he did not get a job soon. Miguel was sad.

When he walked inside, he could feel the hot air that had built up in the apartment all day with the windows closed. He opened all the windows and sat in a chair next to a window that faced the street. Miguel was tired, but he took out his violin and began to play sad, beautiful music.

The music sounded very sad, but it made Miguel feel calm. He played for a long time. He thought of his mother and how the music would have made her cry.

An hour went by as Miguel played his violin, and he did not even know the time had passed. At last he put down his violin and felt a little better.

Miguel looked out the window. He saw a man standing against a street lamp, looking up at him. The man began clapping. Miguel did not know what to think of this, but the man just kept on clapping.

"My good man," called the man from the street. "I am clapping because your music was the most beautiful music I have heard in a long time. May I speak with you?"

Miguel walked down the stairs to meet the man. The two of them shook hands as the man said, "I want you to work for me. I make movies. You can play your violin at my studio when I make movies. My name is Charlie. Charlie Chaplin."

Miguel could not believe it! "You are Charlie Chaplin?" he asked.

This man did not look like the man Miguel had seen so often on the movie screen. Where were his hat, his dirty topcoat, and his big shoes?

"I am," said the man. "As I walked by, I heard you playing the violin. I have been looking for something to help the actors cry in my next movie. Your sad music will help."

"Cry?" asked Miguel.

"Yes, there is a very sad part in the movie. I would like you to play your sad music as we make that part," said Charlie Chaplin. "It sounded so beautiful that I am sure my actors will cry when they hear it. It will help my movie. Will you work for me?"

"I would be happy to!" said Miguel.

Miguel had come to Hollywood to be an actor but found a job as a violin player. He did not care, though. His dream had come true. He was going to work with Charlie Chaplin!

Mrs. Gibson Puts on a Show

A large crowd sat in the wood stands around Lambert Field in St. Louis, Missouri. But the crowd was not as large as Mrs. R. J. Gibson had expected. On such a nice summer day, she had thought more people would be in the stands.

But Mrs. R. J. Gibson still would make quite a lot of money from the people who did pay for seats, so she put those thoughts out of her head and sat back to watch the show.

The air show was set to begin very soon. There was much excitement as the crowd waited to watch pilots do all kinds of tricks with airplanes high in the sky. Airplanes were still new to many people around the country. Some people still called them "flying machines."

Airplane tricks were difficult and full of real danger. It was 1924, and airplanes were not very safe yet. Pilots would often take great chances with their lives to put on a great show.

Of course the pilots always thought they would be safe. But people who ran air shows had seen many tricks in the air. And they knew what happened to pilots when tricks went wrong.

Mrs. R. J. Gibson always said, “On one hand, airplane tricks are not as dangerous as most people in the stands think. On the other hand, the tricks are never as safe as most pilots think.” She knew a lot about airplanes and pilots.

The weather today was clear. The sun was bright, and the winds were calm. It was good flying weather.

The only thing the pilots would have to worry much about was the sun. Looking at the sun could blind the pilots for several seconds, and that was very dangerous.

Even though Mrs. R. J. Gibson did worry a lot about her pilots and their dangerous tricks, she still put on the shows every weekend. The big reason she put on air shows was to make money. But she put on shows for another reason too. She wanted people in the crowds to see what good airplanes and great pilots could do together.

Like most people who loved airplanes, Mrs. R. J. Gibson thought flying had a great future. Many airplanes were already carrying mail across the United States. Many more would carry mail in the future.

And as airplanes got better, they would carry people all over the United States too. Some already did.

"Just think of all the time airplanes will save us!" Mrs. R. J. Gibson would often say.

The air shows were also good ways to help young pilots make some money. And even though the pilots did tricks, they were often bright, serious young men and women who knew that flying and airplanes were the way of the future.

One of the most serious pilots was going to fly in Mrs. R. J. Gibson's show in St. Louis today. He could not fly in every show because he also had a job flying airplanes to carry United States mail. But Mrs. R. J. Gibson was always happy when this top pilot was at her show.

The pilot was a tall, calm man. When he was flying in air shows and doing tricks, he was called Beans Lindbergh. His real name was Charles.

Mrs. R. J. Gibson knew Charles Lindbergh had been flying in air shows in Illinois, Colorado, and many other places. He had made a name for himself all over the country. Yet the young pilot always seemed to find his way back to St. Louis.

Beans was a good-looking young man. That helped with the crowds at the show. Mrs. R. J. Gibson always made sure the people in the stands saw Beans's face before he got in his plane and took off.

It was almost 1:00 and time for the show. Mrs. R. J. Gibson climbed up the stands to the booth at the top. She turned on the loudspeaker in the booth.

When the loudspeaker was on, Mrs. R. J. Gibson said hello to the crowd and told them the show was about to start. As they cheered, the people looked to the booth to see who was talking.

People always did that. Mrs. R. J. Gibson was not sure why, but she thought it might be because people were surprised to hear a woman talk on a loudspeaker. She always laughed to herself when she thought about their surprise. She knew then that people would be even more surprised when they saw who the first pilot would be.

“Good people of St. Louis, please give a big hand to the brave and the beautiful Miss Lizzie Nelson,” Mrs. R. J. Gibson said into the loudspeaker.

The crowd cheered again. It was a woman pilot! Some people in the crowd at Mrs. R. J. Gibson’s air shows were always surprised to find that not all pilots were men.

Mrs. R. J. Gibson did not understand their thinking. All a pilot needed was good eyes, a quick mind, and a brave heart. It did not matter at all if a pilot was a man or a woman.

Lizzie Nelson ran in front of the stands, took a bow, and ran to her airplane. In seconds she was in the air.

Lizzie flew straight up to the sun and then made a quick turn straight down. She flew very low over the stands, and the crowd jumped up and cheered.

Lizzie flew her bright yellow airplane in little circles and in big circles. She flew upside down over the stands. She even made an upside-down circle or two.

Lizzie was new to the air show. She did not know many tricks yet, but she was learning. Mrs. R. J. Gibson knew Lizzie soon would be a very good pilot. Soon she might even be the star of the air show.

As Mrs. R. J. Gibson watched Lizzie, she was amazed. Pilots always amazed her. Mrs. R. J. Gibson was not a pilot herself. She had been in airplanes with pilots as they did tricks, but she did not like being there.

Mrs. R. J. Gibson knew she was not as brave as any of the pilots in the air show. And she also knew she would get sick if she flew upside down!

After Lizzie Nelson amazed the crowd with her tricks, the people cheered and cheered. Mrs. R. J. Gibson did too. She always cheered when one of the pilots was safe on the ground. Her worry was over then.

Next in the show was a race between two airplanes. The crowd soon cheered and cheered as the airplanes raced low in front of the stands. At first the crowd did not seem to see that one of the airplanes raced upside down. But soon people in the stands were standing up and pointing at it.

The two airplanes turned around and raced back. This time the other airplane flew upside down.

Then the airplanes raced one more time. This time both airplanes flew upside down. The planes flew so close to each other! The crowd stood up and cheered some more.

Now it was time for the star of the show, Beans Lindbergh.

Beans shook hands with people in the front row of the stands. Mrs. R. J. Gibson wanted the people to see his good-looking face up close.

When Beans jumped into his airplane, the crowd was clapping already. As his airplane climbed high in the sky, the people cheered and cheered!

As Mrs. R. J. Gibson watched Beans, she worried. She always worried about all the pilots, but she worried about Beans the most.

Beans was the best pilot she had ever seen. Mrs. R. J. Gibson thought he might do something great with an airplane one day. But the tricks this serious young man did were so dangerous that she worried he might never get a chance to do more.

Mrs. R. J. Gibson worried today as Beans started the one trick that made her most afraid.

As Beans flew high in the sky, his airplane's engine roared. Many people in the crowd covered their ears. Beans just flew higher and higher.

The sun was so bright that people in the stands then put their hands above their eyes so they could see the airplane climb higher.

When the airplane looked as though it was as high as it could go, something happened. The roaring of the engine stopped. The airplane stopped climbing in the sky. The engine was not working!

People in the crowd stopped clapping and looked at each other. They were silent as Beans's airplane fell. It tumbled and tumbled in the air. It fell fast and tumbled more. As it got closer to the ground, people in the stands could not watch it anymore.

Then at the last second, Beans turned the engine back on and pulled his airplane out of the fall. He flew over the crowd. It was a trick! The airplane was fine.

One by one the people in the crowd opened their eyes. They could not believe it. The airplane had come so close to the ground!

The crowd began clapping again. “Lindbergh! Lindbergh! Lindbergh!” they cheered.

As the crowd cheered, Mrs. R. J. Gibson opened her eyes too. She had not watched Beans do the trick. She never could.

The Poor Cat!

In the excitement of that summer evening, two questions were never answered. How did the cat get that high up on a bridge in the middle of New York City? And how long was the poor cat up there before Lillian Parks saw it?

Even though the cat was not a kitten, it was very small. Its size and gray color may have made it very hard for people to see on the steel girders of the bridge. Or if people saw the poor cat before Lillian did, they just did not do anything to help it.

But Lillian did something. She would have felt terrible if she had not.

Lillian was on her way home around 5:00 that evening. The bus she was on crossed the bridge on the way to Brooklyn. As the bus neared the Brooklyn end of the bridge, Lillian looked up.

Lillian saw something moving in the bridge's steel girders high above her. She thought it was just a bird at first. Birds often flew on and off the steel girders. She was sure birds had nests up there.

But when Lillian took a good look, she saw it was not a bird. It was cat! Lillian called, “Stop! Stop! The poor cat! There is a cat high up in the bridge girders!”

But the bus driver did not stop. He could not stop on the bridge at 5:00 in the afternoon! He would cause traffic to back up all the way to Manhattan. Then hundreds of people trying to make their way home from work would get very angry.

Lillian walked to the front of the bus and said to the driver, “This is very dangerous! A small cat is high up in the steel girders on the bridge. We must stop so someone can climb up to get it.”

The driver had to watch the traffic, so he could not look up to see whether a cat was in the girders.

“Are you sure it is not a bird?” the driver asked.

“It is not a bird! It is cat! You must stop so we can climb up to save it,” said Lillian.

“If I stop now, I will back up traffic,” said the driver. “And if I do stop, who would climb high onto the bridge to save a cat?”

Lillian had not thought about that, but one way or another she was still going to find a way to save the cat.

Just then the bus stopped. Traffic in front of it was backed up.

"We have stopped," said Lillian. "Please let me off the bus."

The driver opened the door of the bus, and Lillian almost jumped out. She ran back onto the bridge to where she had seen the cat. She had to look a bit until she found the right girder. The cat hid back from the edge of the girder but was looking down.

Lillian looked up at the high girder. She thought she could see the poor little cat looking right at her. Lillian could not hear it over the noise of the traffic, but she could see the cat's little mouth open and close as though it were crying.

The girder reached from the middle of the bridge to the side. Off the side and far below was the East River. The fall from the bridge to the river would be terrible!

The girder crossed high over three lanes of traffic. The traffic in all the lanes was stopped now, as the bus had been. At this time of day,

New York City traffic often stopped on the bridge for several minutes.

Lillian looked at a big truck in one of the lanes. Lillian wondered whether she could climb up on top of the truck and reach up to save the cat.

As she looked at the top of the truck and at the cat and back again, she knew she would need to put three or four trucks on top of each other to reach the cat! The poor thing was that high!

All at once the cars and trucks on the bridge started to move again. Lillian had to do something. Then several yards away in one of the lanes, Lillian saw a police car moving with the traffic.

Lillian jumped up and down and called, "Help! Police! A little cat is in great danger!"

The police officer in the car was not sure what Lillian said, but he pulled up to the side of the bridge next to her. As he got out of the car, Lillian pointed at the girders. "A cat is stuck up there," she said. "We must do something!"

The police officer looked up—way up! A cat *was* stuck in the girders! How did it get there?

"I started working at the police department in 1906," said the officer. "That means I have been on the job for twenty years. And in all that time, I have never seen a cat stuck high up on a bridge! How in the world did your cat ever get up there?"

"Oh, that cat does not belong to me, Officer," said Lillian.

"Well, then who does it belong to?" asked the police officer.

"How should I know?" said Lillian. She was not happy with the officer's questions. There was no time for them. Something had to be done fast. "All I know is that someone needs to save the poor thing!"

The police officer asked another question. "What do you think we should do?"

"Can you climb up and get it?" asked Lillian.

"No," said the officer. "I don't think I can climb that high. But I will call the fire department, and they might."

Then the police officer looked at the traffic on the bridge. "But I had better not call the fire department until some of this traffic has cleared a bit."

Lillian did not want to hear that. "Why?" she asked. "Why do you have to wait until the traffic clears? If we wait too long, it may be too late."

"If a truck from the fire department comes here now, it will cause traffic to back up all across New York City for quite a while—maybe even hours. We cannot do that for a cat!" said the police officer.

Lillian looked up at the cat on the bridge again. The cat was starting to move down the girder to the edge by the river. "Oh, no," Lillian said. She pulled on the police officer's coat and pointed up.

The police officer could tell that the cat could be in real danger. It would be terrible if the poor thing should fall hundreds of feet into the river. But he knew if he called the fire department now, he would be laughed at for the next twenty years.

As the officer thought about what to do, a tall man in work clothes came walking across the bridge.

The tall man had an easy walk that covered a lot of ground fast. He was carrying a lunch box and a newspaper.

When the man got closer, Lillian looked away from the cat for a second and saw the man. Something told Lillian this man could help the poor cat.

"Do you see a cat way up in the bridge there? Do you think you can get that cat from that girder?" she asked as she pointed to the poor cat.

"Sure," said the man as he gave his lunch box and newspaper to Lillian to hold.

The police officer and Lillian looked at the man. He had made it sound as though it would be easy to save the cat. It was as though Lillian had asked him to do something as easy as passing the salt at dinner or buttoning his coat.

The man looked at the bridge. He walked to a girder that went up the side on the edge far above the river. Then he started climbing. When he got to the top of that girder, he was as high as the cat.

Then the man walked on a long girder that led to the girder with the cat. This girder was only a foot wide. On one side of girder was the East River, far, far below. On the other side were the lanes of traffic. They were far below too.

A fall either way would be terrible! But the man did not look worried. He was moving with an easy walk that covered a lot of ground fast. Lillian and the police officer could not believe it!

When the man came to the girder with the cat, he turned and walked the last foot or so to the cat. The man picked up the poor cat and gave it a rub on the head.

Then the tall man turned and walked back the way he had come. As he walked, he talked a little to the cat.

In minutes the tall man was back down on the ground. Lillian gave the man his lunch box and newspaper. The man gave her the cat.

"How did you do that?" asked the police officer.

At first the man did not know what the officer meant. Then the man said, "Oh, you mean walk on the girders? I do that every day on skyscrapers."

Then the officer remembered a newspaper story he had read. "You are one of the Mohawk people who build skyscrapers!" he said.

"Yes, I am a Mohawk, and I help build skyscrapers," said the man with a smile.

The Mohawk people were often seen building large skyscrapers and bridges all over New York and many other places. If the Mohawks were afraid of being up so high on many-story buildings and bridges, they did not show it.

"You are a very brave man," said Lillian. "Thank you for bringing down the cat."

"I was glad to help," said the tall man.

The police officer and Lillian watched as the man left. He had an easy walk that covered a lot of ground fast.